I0521029

Millionaire Mindset

Simple Steps to Wealth in Any Economy

Richard Trillion Mantey

Copyright © 2025

All Rights Reserved

Dedication

To my parents—

Your love, sacrifice, and example planted the first seeds of belief in me.

You taught me the value of hard work, faith, and never settling for less.

And to every dreamer who's ever been told they're not enough—

This book is proof that your mindset is your greatest asset.

Believe bigger, act boldly, and never stop building the life you deserve.

Acknowledgments

First and foremost, I thank God for the wisdom, strength, and inspiration that made this book possible. Without divine guidance, none of this would exist.

To my incredible parents, your unwavering love, sacrifice, and belief in me are the roots of every success I've achieved. You taught me to dream big, work hard, and stay grounded.

To my editors—thank you for helping shape this message with clarity and power. Your thoughtful feedback and sharp eyes elevated every page.

To my readers—you are the reason this book was written. Your desire to grow, rise above limitations, and take control of your future fuels my mission. I am deeply honored to be part of your journey.

To my mentors, friends, and supporters—thank you for your encouragement, your wisdom, and your reminders to keep going even when the path wasn't clear.

And finally, to anyone who has ever doubted their potential or been held back by fear, this book is for you. Your breakthrough begins the moment you choose to believe in the power of your mindset.

With deep gratitude,

Richard Trillion Mantey

About the Author

Richard Trillion Mantey is a success strategist, personal growth author, and entrepreneur dedicated to helping others unlock their full financial and personal potential. With a deep passion for mindset mastery and wealth-building habits, Richard empowers readers to shift their thinking, take focused action, and create lives of lasting impact and abundance.

Through his bestselling books and workshops, Richard has helped thousands of readers reframe their beliefs about money, success, and self-worth. His message is clear: wealth starts in the mind, and with the right mindset, anyone can rise, no matter the economy.

When he's not writing, Richard enjoys studying human potential, mentoring others, and living with purpose, gratitude, and vision.

Contents

Preface

Wealth is not just about money. It's about mindset, habits, and our daily choices shaping our future. Too often, people believe financial success is reserved for the lucky or the privileged. But the truth is simpler: anyone can build wealth with the right mindset, consistent actions, and a willingness to grow.

This book was written to demystify that process. Inside these pages, you'll find real stories, practical steps, and proven strategies you can apply today, no matter your background or the state of the economy. From mastering daily routines to setting clear goals, from overcoming limiting beliefs to building resilience, each chapter is designed to give you tools that work in real life. My goal is simple: to help you think bigger, act boldly, and build lasting wealth on a solid foundation of mindset and action.

Your journey doesn't start with money; it starts with how you think. And it starts now.

Chapter 1: The Foundation of a Millionaire Mindset

Understanding Wealth and Abundance

Understanding wealth and abundance begins with recognising that they are not merely financial constructs, but rather states of mind. Many individuals mistakenly believe that wealth is solely about accumulating money. However, true abundance encompasses a broader spectrum, including mental, emotional, and social richness. A compelling story that illustrates this concept is that of John, a man who lived in a modest home but was surrounded by a loving family and supportive friends. Despite not being wealthy in the traditional sense, John felt an overwhelming sense of abundance in his life, demonstrating that the mindset we adopt can significantly influence our perception of wealth.

Scientific research supports the idea that our beliefs directly impact our financial outcomes. Studies show that individuals who possess a positive money mindset are more likely to engage in behaviours that lead to greater financial success. This aligns with the principles of neuroplasticity, which highlight our brain's ability to reorganise itself based on our thoughts and actions. By cultivating a mindset of abundance, we can rewire our brains to attract opportunities rather than obstacles, enabling us to thrive in any economy.

To foster a millionaire mindset, it is essential to adopt specific habits that promote wealth and abundance. One effective step is to practice gratitude regularly. A simple exercise such as writing down three things you are grateful for each day can shift your focus from scarcity to abundance. This practice not only enhances emotional well-being but also opens your mind to new possibilities. In turn, being grateful creates a positive feedback loop that encourages further abundance in various aspects of life, including finances.

Another crucial step is to surround yourself with like-minded individuals who embody the wealth and abundance mindset. This could involve joining networking groups, attending seminars, or simply engaging with friends who inspire you to grow. The power of community cannot be underestimated; when we connect with others who share our aspirations, we are more likely to stay motivated and accountable. This collective energy fosters an environment where success becomes a shared goal, reinforcing the belief that we can achieve wealth together.

Finally, taking calculated risks is an integral part of embracing wealth and abundance. Many successful entrepreneurs have stories of failure before achieving their goals. For instance, J.K. Rowling faced numerous rejections before publishing the Harry Potter series, which ultimately made her one of the wealthiest authors in history. Such narratives remind us that the journey to wealth often involves setbacks, but maintaining a mindset of abundance means viewing these challenges as opportunities for growth. By understanding wealth and abundance in this comprehensive manner, we can pave our own paths to financial success, regardless of the economic climate.

The Power of Mindset in Financial Success

The journey to financial success begins with the right mindset. Many individuals fail to realise that their thoughts and beliefs about money significantly influence their financial outcomes. A powerful mindset can transform how we approach challenges, view opportunities, and ultimately, how we achieve wealth. For instance, consider the story of a young entrepreneur who started with nothing but a belief in her vision. Through persistence and a positive outlook, she overcame numerous obstacles, turning her small startup into a thriving business. This illustrates that financial success often starts in the mind before it manifests in the bank account.

Research supports the idea that mindset plays a crucial role in financial achievements. Studies have shown that individuals who adopt a growth mindset are more likely to embrace challenges and learn from failures rather than fear them. This adaptability is essential in today's ever-changing economic landscape. Those who believe they can improve their financial situation tend to seek out resources, develop skills, and take calculated risks, paving their way to wealth. A prime example is the story of a man who lost everything during a recession. Instead of giving up, he adopted a growth mindset, learned new skills, and eventually rebuilt his fortune.

To cultivate a millionaire mindset, one must take deliberate steps. First, start by identifying and challenging any limiting beliefs you hold about money. This can involve journaling or discussing these beliefs with a mentor or financial coach. Next, practice gratitude for what you have, as this fosters a positive outlook that attracts more financial opportunities. Visualisation techniques can also be helpful; envisioning your financial goals can reinforce your commitment to achieving them. These steps are not just theoretical; they have been successfully employed by countless individuals on their journeys to wealth.

In addition to personal stories and scientific research, it is essential to understand the role of habits in shaping our mindset. Developing daily routines that focus on financial education, such as reading books on wealth creation or listening to podcasts by successful entrepreneurs, can significantly impact your mindset. For example, the habit of setting aside a portion of income for savings or investments creates a sense of discipline and reinforces the belief that wealth is attainable. Over time, these small habits accumulate and contribute to a solid financial foundation.

Ultimately, the power of mindset in financial success cannot be overstated. It is the lens through which we view our capabilities and opportunities. When we cultivate a mindset geared towards growth and success, we open ourselves to a world of possibilities. Remember that every wealthy individual once started where you are now. With the right mindset, determination, and actionable steps, anyone can achieve financial success, regardless of their current situation. The journey is not just about accumulating wealth but transforming the way we think about and interact with money.

Overcoming Limiting Beliefs

Many people are held back by limiting beliefs, which are often deeply ingrained thoughts that convince us we are not capable of achieving our goals. These beliefs can stem from past experiences, societal expectations, or negative feedback from others. For instance, consider Sarah, a talented artist who believed she could never sell her work because her family always told her that pursuing art was a foolish dream. It wasn't until she began to challenge that belief and take small steps toward showcasing her art that she realised her potential. By sharing her journey, she inspires others to confront their own limiting beliefs.

The science behind limiting beliefs lies in the way our brains are wired. Cognitive behavioural therapy (CBT) shows that our thoughts, feelings, and behaviours are interconnected. When we hold on to negative beliefs, they shape our emotions and actions in ways that can prevent us from pursuing opportunities. By reprogramming our thought patterns, we can create a more empowering narrative. For example, when John, an entrepreneur, faced multiple failures, he chose to view each setback as a learning opportunity rather than a sign of inadequacy. This shift in perspective not only boosted his confidence but ultimately led him to success in his ventures.

To overcome limiting beliefs, it's essential to take actionable steps. Start by identifying specific beliefs that are holding you back. Write them down and reflect on their origins. For instance, if you believe that you are not good with money, ask yourself why you feel this way. Often, these beliefs are based on misinformation or past experiences rather than fact. Next, challenge these thoughts by gathering evidence that contradicts them. This could involve seeking advice from financial experts or learning about successful individuals who overcame similar challenges.

Another effective strategy is to surround yourself with positive influences. The people we spend time with can significantly impact our mindset. Join groups or communities where individuals share your aspirations, and engage with those who have successfully overcome their limiting beliefs. Tara, a business coach, found that by networking with like-minded individuals, she was able to replace her self-doubt with encouragement and inspiration. This environment can foster growth and provide the support necessary to break free from limiting beliefs.

Finally, practise self-compassion and patience. Overcoming limiting beliefs is not an overnight process; it requires consistent effort and a willingness to embrace discomfort. Celebrate small victories along the way, and remind yourself that setbacks are part of the journey. As you slowly dismantle these beliefs, you will find that your potential is far greater than you ever imagined. In doing so, you not only pave the way for your success but also inspire others to challenge their own limiting beliefs, creating a ripple effect of empowerment and growth.

Chapter 2: The Billion Dollar Habit

Cultivating Daily Success Rituals

Cultivating daily success rituals is essential for achieving wealth and prosperity in any economy. The most successful individuals often share one common trait: they have established routines that set them up for success each day. These rituals, whether it's a morning meditation, journaling, or a strategic planning session, help to focus their minds and intentions, making them more productive and effective in their pursuits. By implementing these practices, anyone can start to shift their mindset towards one of abundance and achievement.

Take, for example, the story of a young entrepreneur who transformed her life by waking up an hour earlier each day. She dedicated this time to reflect on her goals, read motivational literature, and outline her tasks for the day. Over time, this simple morning routine not only increased her productivity but also instilled a sense of purpose and clarity. It allowed her to approach challenges with a positive mindset, ultimately leading her to build a successful business from the ground up.

Science backs up the effectiveness of daily rituals as well. Research has shown that habits form the foundation of our actions and can significantly influence our thoughts and behaviours. According to psychologists, establishing a routine can lead to improved mental health, increased self-discipline, and enhanced performance. By consciously choosing to engage in productive rituals, individuals can rewire their brains to prioritise success, making it easier to overcome obstacles and stay motivated.

To cultivate your own daily success rituals, start by identifying activities that resonate with you. Consider incorporating elements such as gratitude exercises, exercise, or skill development into your routine. Set aside a specific time each day dedicated to these activities, and be consistent. Over time, as these rituals become ingrained in your daily life, you will likely notice a shift in your mindset as well as your overall success.

In conclusion, cultivating daily success rituals is a powerful step towards achieving wealth and fulfilling your potential. By learning from the stories of others and leveraging scientific insights, anyone can develop habits that foster a millionaire mindset. Remember, it is not about the complexity of the rituals but their consistency and alignment with your goals that will ultimately pave the way for success.

The Importance of Consistency

Consistency is the cornerstone of success in any endeavour, especially when it comes to building wealth. Imagine a young entrepreneur who wakes up every day at 5 a.m. to work on his business. He dedicates an hour each morning to learning about his industry, honing his skills, and strategising for the day ahead. This daily commitment, though seemingly small, compounds over time, leading to significant growth. It is this daily practice of consistency that separates the successful from those who merely dream of success.

Science backs the power of consistency. Research shows that habits are formed through repeated actions, and the more consistent we are, the more these actions become second nature. For instance, a study published in the European Journal of Social Psychology found that it takes an average of 66 days to form a new habit. This means that if you commit to a positive behaviour, like saving a percentage of your income, it will eventually become a part of your lifestyle. The key is persistence; every small effort counts and builds towards a larger goal.

Consider the story of a man who decided to save just one dollar a day. At first, it seemed trivial, but he remained committed. Over the course of a year, he discovered that he had saved over $365. This simple act of consistency not only provided him with a financial cushion but also instilled a mindset of abundance. He began to apply the same principle to other areas of his life, leading to improvements in his health, relationships, and career. This illustrates how small, consistent actions can lead to substantial changes over time.

For anyone looking to adopt a millionaire mindset, it is essential to establish consistent habits. Start by identifying one or two areas where you can improve your daily routine. Whether it's budgeting, networking, or personal development, make a commitment to engage in these activities regularly. Track your progress and celebrate small victories along the way. Remember, consistency does not mean perfection; it's about showing up and making an effort, even on days when motivation is low.

In conclusion, the importance of consistency cannot be overstated. It is the driving force that transforms aspirations into reality. By committing to consistent actions, you create a framework for growth, learning, and ultimately, wealth. As you embark on your journey towards financial success, remember that every step counts, and with unwavering commitment, you can cultivate the habits that lead to greatness.

Building Resilience Against Setbacks

Building resilience against setbacks is a crucial skill for anyone striving for success. Life is filled with challenges and obstacles, but how we respond to these setbacks can define our path to wealth and achievement. Just like the story of Thomas Edison, who faced thousands of failures before inventing the light bulb, embracing setbacks as learning opportunities can transform our mindset. Edison's resilience exemplifies the importance of persistence and a positive outlook in the face of adversity.

Science supports the notion that resilience can be cultivated through practice and mindset shifts. Research in psychology shows that individuals who view setbacks as temporary and surmountable are more likely to bounce back. This growth mindset allows us to approach failures with curiosity rather than despair. By reframing our thoughts, we can learn valuable lessons and adapt our strategies, ultimately leading to greater success in our endeavours.

To build resilience, it is essential to develop certain habits and strategies. Setting realistic goals is the first step; by breaking larger objectives into smaller, manageable tasks, we can maintain motivation even when faced with difficulties. Additionally, surrounding ourselves with a supportive network can provide encouragement during tough times. Sharing our experiences with others who have faced similar challenges can also foster a sense of community and understanding.

Another vital aspect of resilience is self-care. Taking time to recharge and reflect allows us to maintain our mental and emotional health. Whether through exercise, meditation, or simply enjoying a hobby, prioritising self-care helps us approach setbacks with a clear mind and renewed energy. It is essential to remember that taking breaks does not signify weakness but rather a strategic step towards long-term success.

Ultimately, building resilience against setbacks is a journey that requires continuous effort and dedication. By adopting a positive mindset, developing practical strategies, and prioritising self-care, we can navigate the inevitable challenges on our path to success. Just as a tree bends with the wind but does not break, we too can learn to adapt and thrive, turning our setbacks into stepping stones towards our goals.

Chapter 3: Setting Clear Financial Goals

Defining Your Vision of Wealth

Defining your vision of wealth is the first crucial step towards achieving it. Many people chase money without understanding what wealth truly means to them. For some, wealth is about financial freedom to travel the world, while for others, it may mean having the time to spend with family. Before embarking on your journey to wealth, take a moment to define what it means to you personally. This vision will serve as your guiding star, keeping you focused and motivated.

Consider the story of Sarah, a teacher who always dreamed of opening her own school. For years, she felt trapped in her job, longing for a more fulfilling life. One day, she took a step back and defined her vision of wealth—not just in terms of money, but as having the ability to make a difference in her community. With this new perspective, she was able to save diligently and eventually opened her school, transforming her life and the lives of her students. Sarah's story illustrates the power of defining wealth beyond mere financial gain.

Science supports the idea that having a clear vision can lead to success. Research shows that individuals who set specific goals are more likely to achieve them. When you define your vision of wealth, you create a mental picture that influences your decisions and actions. This mental imagery activates the brain's reward system, making the pursuit of your goals more fulfilling. As you visualise your success, you build a roadmap that guides your journey, making it easier to navigate challenges along the way.

To develop your vision of wealth, follow these simple steps. First, reflect on your values and what brings you joy. Write down your thoughts and create a vision board that encapsulates your goals and dreams. Next, share your vision with trusted friends or mentors who can provide support and accountability. Lastly, make a habit of revisiting and refining your vision regularly as you grow and evolve. This ongoing process will keep you aligned with your true desires and help you stay motivated on your path to success.

Remember, defining your vision of wealth is not a one-time exercise; it is an evolving journey. Embrace the changes in your life and allow your vision to adapt as you discover new passions and opportunities. By staying true to your personal definition of wealth, you will cultivate a millionaire mindset that empowers you to think, act, and grow rich in any economy.

Creating SMART Goals

Creating SMART goals is an essential step for anyone aiming to cultivate a millionaire mindset. The acronym SMART stands for Specific, Measurable, Achievable, Relevant, and Time-bound. When you define your goals using these criteria, you clarify your ambitions and enhance your focus. For instance, instead of saying, "I want to save money," you could state, "I will save £5,000 in the next 12 months by setting aside £400 each month." This specificity not only makes your goal more tangible but also motivates you to take consistent action.

The science behind goal setting reveals that having clear, structured goals significantly increases the likelihood of success. Research shows that individuals who write down their goals are 42% more likely to achieve them. This phenomenon can be attributed to the psychological commitment that comes from articulating your desires. Sharing your goals with a trusted friend or colleague can further enhance accountability, making your journey towards wealth not just a personal endeavour but a shared experience.

Consider the story of a young entrepreneur who transformed his life by applying the SMART framework. Initially overwhelmed by the idea of starting a business, he set a goal to launch his online store within six months. By breaking down this goal into smaller tasks—conducting market research, sourcing products, and building a website—he turned an abstract dream into a concrete plan. With each mini-goal achieved, his confidence grew, ultimately leading to the successful launch of his business and financial independence.

Implementing SMART goals involves a step-by-step approach. First, identify what you truly want to achieve. Next, ensure that your goal is specific and measurable; clarity is key. Then, assess whether your goal is achievable and relevant to your broader life aspirations. Finally, assign a realistic timeframe to your goal. This step-by-step process not only simplifies your ambitions but also creates a roadmap that guides you towards your destination.

In conclusion, creating SMART goals is a powerful tool in developing a millionaire mindset. By transforming vague aspirations into specific, actionable steps, you position yourself for success in any economic climate. Remember, the journey to wealth is not merely about the destination but the growth you experience along the way. Embrace the process, remain committed to your goals, and watch as you flourish in both your personal and financial life.

Tracking Progress and Celebrating Milestones

Tracking progress is an essential aspect of achieving wealth and success. By measuring our advancements, we gain insight into what works and what needs adjustment. For instance, consider the story of a small business owner who meticulously tracked her sales each month. Initially, her numbers fluctuated significantly, causing frustration. However, by documenting her progress, she identified peak times and adjusted her marketing strategies accordingly, leading to a remarkable increase in revenue. This demonstrates that awareness of our progress can illuminate pathways to growth.

Celebrating milestones is equally important in maintaining motivation. Achieving a goal, no matter how small, deserves recognition. For example, a young entrepreneur set a target to save a specific amount each month. Upon reaching this target for six consecutive months, she treated herself to a small reward. This act of celebration reinforced her commitment to her financial goals and made the journey enjoyable. Science suggests that celebrating achievements activates the brain's reward system, which can enhance motivation and encourage further progress.

Incorporating systems for tracking and celebrating milestones can be simple yet effective. Keeping a journal or using apps designed for goal tracking can help visualise progress. For instance, a personal finance app might allow users to set savings goals, and as they reach each milestone, the app sends notifications to celebrate their achievements. These small nudges can keep individuals engaged and focused on their financial journey. By utilising technology, we can make the process of tracking not only easier but also more rewarding.

Moreover, sharing milestones with a community can amplify the joy of achievement. Whether it's through social media or local networking groups, sharing successes can inspire others and create a supportive environment. A group of friends might decide to hold monthly meetings where they discuss their financial goals and celebrate each other's successes. Such communal support fosters accountability and encourages everyone to strive for their objectives, reinforcing the idea that wealth-building is a collective journey.

Finally, reflecting on progress and milestones helps solidify lessons learned along the way. Each setback and success contributes to a richer understanding of the wealth-building process. By revisiting past achievements, individuals can recognise patterns that lead to success and those that require change. This reflective practice not only enhances future strategies but also builds resilience. In essence, tracking progress and celebrating milestones are pivotal habits that transform the journey to wealth into a fulfilling and enriching experience.

Chapter 4: The Art of Financial Literacy

Understanding Money Management

Understanding money management is not merely about numbers; it is about cultivating a mindset that appreciates the value of financial resources. Imagine a young entrepreneur, Sarah, who started her journey with just a small amount of savings. She quickly realised that her success wasn't just tied to her initial investment, but to her ability to manage that money wisely. By learning to allocate her funds effectively, she transformed her modest savings into a thriving business, showcasing how the right mindset can lead to financial abundance.

The science behind money management stresses the importance of budgeting and saving. Research indicates that individuals who create and adhere to a budget are more likely to achieve their financial goals. Consider the story of John, who meticulously tracked his spending habits each month. This simple act not only helped him identify unnecessary expenses but also enabled him to save consistently. John's disciplined approach to money management allowed him to invest in opportunities that ultimately expanded his wealth.

Emotional intelligence plays a crucial role in money management. People often make financial decisions based on emotions rather than logic, leading to poor choices. Take the example of Lisa, who, after experiencing a financial setback, felt overwhelmed and anxious. Instead of succumbing to fear, she sought advice and re-evaluated her financial strategies. By understanding her emotional triggers, she learned to make decisions grounded in rationality, which paved the way for her financial recovery.

Steps to effective money management can be straightforward yet powerful. Establishing clear financial goals is the first step—knowing what you want to achieve helps direct your efforts. Next, create a realistic budget that aligns with those goals. Finally, monitor your progress regularly and adjust as necessary. This process is akin to training for a marathon; you need a plan, dedication, and the ability to adapt to changing circumstances.

In conclusion, understanding money management is a multifaceted journey that involves knowledge, emotional awareness, and practical steps. By embracing these principles, anyone can cultivate a millionaire mindset. Whether it's through the inspiring stories of others or the science of financial habits, the path to wealth is accessible to all who are willing to learn and grow. It's not just about making money; it's about making informed decisions that lead to a prosperous future.

Investing Basics for Beginners

Investing can seem daunting, especially for beginners. However, understanding the basics is essential for building wealth. Imagine a young woman named Sarah, who, despite her modest income, decided to invest a small portion of her earnings every month. Over time, the power of compound interest transformed her savings into a significant nest egg, demonstrating that anyone can start with little and grow it into much more.

To grasp the fundamentals of investing, one must first understand the different types of investment vehicles available. Stocks, bonds, real estate, and mutual funds each have unique characteristics and risk profiles. Consider John, who invested in a diversified portfolio of these assets. By balancing his investments, he not only mitigated risks but also maximised his potential for returns, showcasing the importance of diversification in an investment strategy.

Another critical aspect to consider is the concept of time. The earlier you start investing, the more time your money has to grow. A powerful story is that of a college student who began investing small amounts while still in school. By the time he graduated, his initial investments had significantly appreciated in value, illustrating how starting early can yield substantial benefits. Time is truly a friend to those who invest wisely.

Emotion can also play a significant role in investing. It's easy to get swept up in market trends, leading to impulsive decisions. For instance, during a market downturn, many investors panic and sell their shares, often at a loss. However, those who maintain a clear focus on their long-term goals, much like Emma, who weathered several market fluctuations and ultimately emerged wealthier, understand that patience and perseverance are key traits of successful investors.

Finally, educating oneself continuously is paramount in the journey of investing. The financial landscape is ever-changing, and staying informed can make all the difference. Consider the story of a man who, after years of little progress, committed to learning about investing through books and seminars. His newfound knowledge empowered him to make informed decisions, ultimately leading to financial freedom. By investing in education as much as in assets, anyone can cultivate a millionaire mindset and thrive in any economy.

The Role of Financial Education

Financial education serves as the cornerstone of achieving wealth and prosperity in any economy. It is not merely about understanding numbers and spreadsheets; it is about developing a mindset that embraces opportunities and navigates challenges with confidence. Consider the story of a young woman, Maria, who grew up in a low-income household. With limited access to financial resources, she faced obstacles that seemed insurmountable. However, by seeking financial education through community workshops, she learned to budget effectively, invest wisely, and ultimately built a successful business. Her journey exemplifies how financial literacy can transform lives irrespective of one's starting point.

Research consistently shows that those with financial education tend to make better financial decisions. A study conducted by the National Endowment for Financial Education found that individuals who received financial education were more likely to save and invest than those who did not. This scientific backing highlights the importance of equipping ourselves and future generations with the necessary tools to make informed choices about money. By understanding concepts like compound interest, risk management, and investment strategies, individuals can create a stable financial future for themselves and their families.

To cultivate a millionaire mindset, it is crucial to adopt specific habits that foster financial growth. Start by setting clear financial goals, whether it's saving for a home, retirement, or starting a business. Break these goals down into actionable steps, such as creating a monthly budget or learning about different investment vehicles. Consistency is key; by making small, daily decisions that align with your financial objectives, you will gradually build a positive habit that contributes to long-term wealth accumulation.

Moreover, embracing a growth mindset is essential in the realm of financial education. Instead of viewing setbacks as failures, perceive them as opportunities for learning. When Mark, a budding entrepreneur, faced a business failure, he did not give up; instead, he analysed his mistakes and sought mentorship to improve his skills. This resilience and willingness to learn not only helped him recover but also propelled him to greater heights in his subsequent ventures. Developing a mindset that welcomes learning and adaptation is vital for anyone aspiring to achieve financial success.

In conclusion, financial education is a powerful tool that can empower individuals to take control of their financial destinies. By sharing knowledge and experiences, we can create a more financially literate society that thrives regardless of economic conditions. Each person's journey will be unique, yet the principles of financial education remain universal. Let us champion the cause of financial literacy and inspire each other to build a prosperous future, one informed decision at a time.

Chapter 5: Developing a Success-Oriented Routine

Morning Rituals of Successful People

Morning rituals are more than just a series of tasks; they are the foundation upon which successful individuals build their lives. Many of the wealthiest and most influential people in the world start their day with intention. For instance, Apple CEO Tim Cook rises at 3:45 am, dedicating time to exercise and plan his day. This early start allows him to tackle challenges with a clear mind. Research has shown that morning routines can significantly impact productivity, helping individuals to harness their focus and set a positive tone for the day ahead.

Another notable example is Richard Branson, who begins his mornings with fitness, often engaging in activities like kitesurfing or running. His belief in the power of physical activity not only energises him but also sparks creativity. Science supports this notion, indicating that exercise releases endorphins, improving mood and cognitive function. By incorporating physical activity into the morning routine, one can foster both mental and physical health, key components for achieving success.

Successful people often include mindfulness practices in their morning rituals. Oprah Winfrey, for instance, dedicates time to meditation, reflecting on her intentions for the day. This practice of mindfulness helps to reduce stress and enhance clarity, allowing her to approach each day with a sense of purpose. Studies have shown that mindfulness can enhance emotional intelligence, a crucial skill for leaders and entrepreneurs alike. By taking just a few moments each morning to centre oneself, anyone can improve their focus and decision-making capabilities.

Additionally, many successful individuals prioritise learning during their mornings. For example, Elon Musk is known to read extensively, often diving into books that expand his knowledge and inspire innovation. Engaging with new information each day can stimulate creativity and critical thinking. Incorporating reading or learning into your morning routine can open doors to new ideas and perspectives, essential for anyone looking to thrive in a competitive landscape.

Lastly, setting goals is a common thread among the morning rituals of successful people. They often take time to write down their objectives for the day, ensuring they remain focused and accountable. This simple yet effective practice can transform one's approach to daily tasks, fostering a proactive mindset. By incorporating goal-setting into your morning routine, you can create a roadmap for success, making it easier to achieve your long-term aspirations. The consistency of these rituals not only builds discipline but also cultivates a millionaire mindset, ready to seize opportunities in any economy.

Time Management Strategies

Time management is not just about organising your schedule; it is about maximising your potential and creating opportunities for wealth. Consider the story of a successful entrepreneur who, despite his humble beginnings, turned his life around by mastering the art of time management. He would rise before dawn, outlining his goals for the day while the world was still asleep. This simple habit allowed him to focus on what truly mattered, turning routine tasks into stepping stones for success.

Research shows that effective time management can significantly enhance productivity and reduce stress. Studies conducted by psychologists reveal that individuals who plan their day are more likely to achieve their goals. By allocating specific time slots for tasks and setting deadlines, you can create a sense of urgency that propels you forward. The science behind this strategy lies in the way our brains respond to structured planning; it activates areas associated with motivation and reward, making it easier to take action and avoid procrastination.

One practical step to improve your time management is to adopt the "Pomodoro Technique," which involves working in focused bursts followed by short breaks. This method not only increases concentration but also gives you the necessary downtime to recharge. Imagine a writer who uses this technique: she sets a timer for 25 minutes, immerses herself in her work, and then takes a five-minute break to refresh her mind. This approach leads to higher productivity and a more enjoyable work experience, ultimately contributing to her financial success.

Furthermore, prioritising tasks is crucial. The Eisenhower Matrix, a simple tool, can help differentiate between what is urgent and what is important. By categorising tasks into these four quadrants, you can focus on high-impact activities that drive your success. For example, a business leader might spend her mornings tackling strategic planning—an important yet often neglected aspect, rather than getting bogged down in minor daily tasks that yield little results.

In conclusion, mastering time management is a vital skill for anyone aspiring to wealth and success. It requires commitment and practice, but the benefits are profound. By implementing these strategies—like early rising, structured planning, focused work sessions, and task prioritisation—you can transform your life. The journey to becoming a millionaire begins with how you manage your time, and the steps you take today will pave the way for your future achievements.

Prioritising Tasks for Maximum Impact

In today's fast-paced world, the ability to prioritise tasks effectively is a skill that can lead to significant success. Many people find themselves overwhelmed by a never-ending to-do list, often failing to distinguish between what is urgent and what is truly important. By focusing on high-impact tasks, individuals can not only enhance their productivity but also align their efforts with their overarching goals. For instance, consider the story of a budding entrepreneur who spent countless hours on minor administrative tasks, neglecting the strategic partnerships that could have propelled his business to new heights. By learning to prioritise, he shifted his focus and unlocked a path to success.

The science behind prioritisation is rooted in understanding our cognitive limitations. Research shows that the human brain can handle only a limited number of simultaneous tasks, with diminishing returns on efficiency as we spread ourselves too thin. By employing techniques such as the Eisenhower Matrix, individuals can categorise tasks into four quadrants: urgent and important, important but not urgent, urgent but not important, and neither. This method empowers individuals to identify which tasks deserve their immediate attention and which can be delegated or deferred, ensuring that their energy is directed towards activities that yield the highest return on investment.

Incorporating stories of successful individuals who have mastered the art of prioritisation can further illustrate its importance. Take, for instance, the renowned author who, upon realising that writing was the key to her wealth, scheduled uninterrupted blocks of time solely for this purpose. By prioritising her writing over other distractions, she produced a bestselling novel that changed her financial trajectory forever. Her story serves as a powerful reminder that prioritising what truly matters can lead to transformative outcomes.

To effectively prioritise tasks for maximum impact, individuals can adopt a structured approach. Start by listing all tasks and categorising them based on urgency and importance. Next, rank these tasks and allocate specific time blocks for their completion. This not only creates a clear roadmap but also instils a sense of accountability. Regularly reviewing this list can help adjust priorities based on evolving circumstances, ensuring that one remains agile and responsive in a dynamic environment.

Ultimately, prioritising tasks is not just about getting more done; it's about making strategic choices that align with one's values and goals. It requires discipline and introspection to continuously assess what actions will lead to the most significant impact. By embracing this mindset, anyone can cultivate the habits necessary for achieving wealth and success, regardless of the challenges they face. The journey to a millionaire mindset begins with the simple, yet powerful, act of prioritising effectively in everyday life.

Chapter 6: Networking and Building Relationships

The Value of Connections

In the journey towards wealth and success, the value of connections cannot be overstated. Each relationship we cultivate acts as a building block for our future. Consider the story of a young entrepreneur who, despite facing numerous challenges, managed to build a thriving business through the power of networking. By attending events, reaching out to mentors, and actively engaging with his community, he transformed his life and outlook. This illustrates that connections are not just beneficial; they are essential for growth.

Science supports this notion, highlighting the importance of social capital in achieving financial success. Studies have shown that individuals with robust networks are more likely to access opportunities that others may miss. The connections we create often provide insights, resources, and support that can propel us forward. By understanding the science behind connections, we can learn to leverage them effectively, turning acquaintances into allies in our quest for wealth.

To harness the power of connections, we must take deliberate steps. First, identify key individuals in your field who inspire you or share your goals. Next, engage with them authentically—whether through social media, professional gatherings, or mutual contacts. Building genuine relationships requires effort and sincerity, but the rewards can be significant. Remember, every connection has the potential to lead to new opportunities or partnerships that could change your trajectory.

Additionally, maintaining these connections is just as crucial as creating them. Regular communication, offering help, and showing appreciation can strengthen bonds over time. Consider the case of a successful investor who often credits his wealth to the relationships he nurtured throughout his career. By consistently engaging with his network, he not only cultivated trust but also gained invaluable insights that contributed to his financial success.

In summary, the value of connections lies in their ability to open doors and expand horizons. As we work towards a millionaire mindset, let us embrace the importance of building and maintaining relationships. By fostering a network that supports our ambitions, we lay the groundwork for lasting success in any economy. Remember, the people we connect with today can significantly impact our journey tomorrow.

Effective Networking Strategies

Effective networking is a cornerstone of achieving success and wealth in any economy. Many individuals overlook the power of building genuine connections, believing that success is solely based on personal effort. However, stories abound of millionaires who credit their success to the relationships they cultivated along their journey. For instance, consider Richard Branson, who often emphasises the importance of networking in his entrepreneurial ventures. He has built a global empire not just on his innovative ideas but also on the partnerships and friendships he forged over the years.

Science supports the notion that networking can significantly influence our success. Research indicates that individuals who actively engage in networking are more likely to discover opportunities, gain insights, and access resources that can propel their careers. This is not merely about exchanging business cards; it's about forming meaningful relationships that can lead to collaboration and mutual support. A study from Harvard found that the most successful individuals often have extensive networks, which they leverage to navigate challenges and seize new opportunities.

To effectively network, one must start by adopting a mindset of generosity. Approach networking not as a transactional exchange, but as an opportunity to help others. This can be as simple as offering advice, sharing resources, or making introductions. By giving first, you create a foundation of trust and respect, which can lead to reciprocal support. Remember the story of a young entrepreneur who volunteered to assist a local charity; through this act, they met influential business leaders who later became mentors and collaborators, illustrating the power of selfless networking.

Another vital strategy is to be intentional about your networking efforts. Attend events, join professional associations, and participate in community initiatives that align with your goals. Set specific networking goals, such as meeting a certain number of new contacts each month or deepening existing relationships. For example, a successful businesswoman once set a goal to connect with five new people each month, leading to a flourishing network that opened doors to countless opportunities. Being proactive in your networking efforts can significantly impact your professional journey.

Lastly, follow up and nurture your connections. After meeting someone, send a personalised message thanking them for their time and expressing your interest in staying in touch. Consistent communication helps keep relationships alive and can lead to collaborations down the line. A successful investor once shared that they make it a point to follow up with every new contact within 48 hours, ensuring that the connection remains fresh. By implementing these strategies, you can harness the power of networking to elevate your success and wealth in any economy.

Nurturing Professional Relationships

Nurturing professional relationships is akin to nurturing a garden; it requires patience, care, and the right environment to flourish. In the world of business and wealth creation, these relationships can be the fertile soil from which opportunities sprout. For instance, consider the story of a young entrepreneur who, through a chance meeting at a networking event, connected with a seasoned investor. That single interaction not only led to funding for her startup but also to invaluable mentorship that shaped her career. Building a network isn't just about collecting contacts; it's about fostering genuine connections that can uplift and inspire.

The science behind professional relationships is compelling. Research shows that people who invest time in networking tend to experience greater career satisfaction and success. A study published in the Journal of Applied Psychology found that strong workplace relationships can lead to increased productivity and job satisfaction. This psychological backing reinforces the idea that when you nurture your connections, you are not only enhancing your personal brand but also paving the way for collaborative ventures that can lead to mutual growth. Investing in these connections can yield dividends that far exceed the initial effort.

To effectively nurture these relationships, it is essential to adopt a mindset of giving rather than taking. This involves actively listening to others, offering help without expecting anything in return, and showing genuine interest in their success. Take the example of a successful business leader who makes it a point to mentor young professionals. By doing so, he not only contributes to their growth but also strengthens his own network. This reciprocal nature of relationships amplifies trust, creating a robust support system that can weather the challenges of any economy.

Moreover, consistent communication is key to maintaining these connections. Regular check-ins, whether through social media, emails, or face-to-face meetings, help keep the relationship alive. For instance, sending a simple note of appreciation or sharing an article relevant to a contact's interests can go a long way in reinforcing the bond. These small gestures demonstrate that you value the relationship, making it more likely that they will reciprocate in times of need. This ongoing dialogue fosters a sense of community and belonging, essential components in the journey towards wealth and success.

In conclusion, nurturing professional relationships is not just a necessary step but a fundamental aspect of achieving a millionaire mindset. By cultivating a network of supportive, like-minded individuals, you create an environment where ideas can flourish and opportunities abound. Whether you're starting out or are already established, remember that success is rarely a solo journey. Embrace the power of connection, and watch as your professional landscape transforms, paving the way for unimaginable growth and success.

Chapter 7: Embracing Risk and Innovation

Understanding the Nature of Risk

Understanding the nature of risk is essential for anyone aspiring to achieve wealth and success. Risk is often viewed with apprehension, yet it is an integral part of the journey towards financial independence. Consider the story of a young entrepreneur who invested his savings into a start-up. Despite the uncertainty, he embraced the risk, applying strategic thinking and resilience. His venture, although fraught with challenges, ultimately led him to success, demonstrating that calculated risks can yield significant rewards.

Scientific research supports the idea that individuals who take measured risks are more likely to achieve their goals. According to behavioural economics, people often underestimate their ability to withstand setbacks. This underestimation can lead to missed opportunities. For instance, a study found that those who viewed failure as a learning experience were more inclined to take risks in the future. This mindset shift is crucial for anyone looking to build wealth, as it allows for growth and adaptation in the face of adversity.

Taking steps to understand and manage risk involves several practical strategies. Firstly, one must perform thorough research and analysis before making financial decisions. This includes assessing potential outcomes and preparing for various scenarios. Secondly, building a support network of mentors and peers can provide valuable insights and encouragement. Sharing experiences can illuminate different approaches to risk management, making it easier to navigate uncertainties.

Moreover, keeping a positive attitude towards risk can transform one's financial journey. Embracing the idea that failure is not the opposite of success but a stepping stone towards it can empower individuals. An inspiring example is a renowned investor who faced multiple failures before achieving monumental success. His story illustrates that resilience in the face of risk is a hallmark of successful individuals, encouraging others to persist despite obstacles.

In conclusion, understanding the nature of risk is not merely about avoiding pitfalls; it's about harnessing the potential for growth. By recognising risk as a companion on the path to wealth, individuals can cultivate a mindset that encourages exploration and innovation. With the right tools and attitudes, anyone can learn to navigate the complexities of risk, ultimately leading to financial success and personal fulfilment.

Innovative Thinking for Business Growth

Innovative thinking is the lifeblood of successful businesses. It enables entrepreneurs to solve problems creatively and to seize opportunities that others may overlook. For instance, consider the story of Airbnb, which transformed the hospitality industry by allowing homeowners to rent out their spare rooms. This innovative approach not only created a new revenue stream for hosts but also provided travellers with unique and affordable accommodation options. Such stories illustrate that thinking outside the box can lead to breakthroughs that drive growth and success.

Science supports the idea that innovative thinking can be nurtured through specific practices. Research indicates that diverse teams often produce more creative solutions than homogenous ones. By bringing together individuals with different backgrounds, experiences, and perspectives, businesses can foster an environment ripe for innovation. Companies like Google have embraced this concept, encouraging collaboration among employees from various departments to generate fresh ideas that propel the business forward.

To cultivate innovative thinking within your own organisation, consider implementing structured brainstorming sessions. These sessions should encourage open dialogue, where every idea is welcomed, regardless of how unconventional it may seem. Subsequently, evaluate these ideas based on their feasibility and potential impact. This process not only empowers employees but also creates a culture of creativity, where individuals feel valued and motivated to contribute their unique insights.

Additionally, embracing a mindset of continuous learning is essential for fostering innovation. Successful entrepreneurs understand that they must remain adaptable and open to new knowledge. This might involve attending workshops, reading industry-related books, or networking with other professionals. For example, Richard Branson, the founder of the Virgin Group, attributes much of his success to his commitment to learning and experimenting with new ideas. This relentless pursuit of knowledge can lead to innovative strategies that keep a business ahead of the competition.

In conclusion, innovative thinking is not just a skill but a crucial habit that can drive business growth. By embracing diversity, encouraging open discussions, and committing to lifelong learning, entrepreneurs can cultivate an environment where creativity flourishes. As you embark on your journey to wealth, remember that the most successful minds are those that dare to think differently, turning challenges into opportunities and ideas into thriving enterprises.

Learning from Failure

Failure is an inevitable part of the journey to success, and understanding how to learn from it can transform one's mindset. Many successful individuals, including renowned entrepreneurs, have faced significant setbacks before achieving greatness. For instance, J.K. Rowling, the author of the Harry Potter series, received numerous rejections before finding a publisher. Her story illustrates that failure is not the end, but rather a stepping stone towards achieving one's dreams. Embracing failure allows us to build resilience and adapt our strategies for future success.

Science backs the notion that learning from failure can enhance our intelligence and creativity. Research indicates that reflecting on our mistakes enables the brain to form new connections and improve problem-solving skills. This cognitive flexibility is crucial in business, where the ability to pivot in response to challenges can mean the difference between success and stagnation. By adopting a growth mindset, we can view failures as opportunities for learning rather than personal shortcomings.

To effectively learn from failure, it is essential to engage in reflective practices. Keeping a journal to document experiences and emotions surrounding failures can provide valuable insights. This process encourages self-awareness and helps identify patterns in our decision-making. Successful individuals often review their failures critically, extracting lessons that inform their future choices. Taking the time to analyse what went wrong not only fosters personal growth but also enhances future business strategies.

Moreover, sharing failure stories with others can create a supportive community where individuals feel empowered to take risks. Networking with like-minded individuals who have experienced setbacks can provide encouragement and new perspectives. These discussions often lead to collaborative problem-solving, where shared experiences can inspire innovative solutions. Remember, every successful entrepreneur has faced their share of failures; it's how they respond that sets them apart.

In conclusion, embracing failure as a learning opportunity is vital for anyone striving for success. By adopting a mindset that values resilience, reflection, and community support, we can navigate the challenges of the entrepreneurial journey with confidence. Ultimately, it is not the failures themselves that define us, but how we choose to rise from them that shapes our path to wealth and success.

Chapter 8: The Role of Mentorship

Finding the Right Mentor

Finding the right mentor is a pivotal step on the journey to financial success and personal growth. Many successful individuals credit their achievements to the guidance and wisdom of a mentor who helped them navigate challenges and seize opportunities. For instance, consider the story of Sara Blakely, founder of Spanx, who attributes much of her success to her mentor, who taught her the value of perseverance and strategic thinking. This demonstrates that a mentor doesn't just provide advice; they also inspire and motivate you to reach your potential.

The science behind mentorship highlights its transformative power. Research shows that having a mentor can significantly enhance your career advancement, increase your confidence, and improve your skill set. A study conducted by the American Society for Training and Development found that 75% of executives credit their success to mentorship. This statistic underscores the importance of finding someone who can guide you, share their insights, and hold you accountable as you pursue your goals.

To find the right mentor, start by identifying what you wish to achieve. Are you looking to improve your financial literacy, enhance your business acumen, or develop a wealth mindset? Once you have clarity on your goals, seek out individuals who have successfully navigated paths similar to yours. Attend industry events, join professional networks, or utilise social media platforms like LinkedIn to connect with potential mentors. Remember, it's crucial to find someone whose values align with yours and who genuinely wants to see you succeed.

Building a relationship with a mentor requires effort and commitment. Approach potential mentors with respect and a clear intention. Share your aspirations and express why you admire their work. It's essential to be open to feedback and willing to take action based on their advice. Additionally, consider offering value in return, whether it's sharing your insights or assisting with projects. This reciprocal relationship can enhance your learning experience and strengthen the bond with your mentor.

Ultimately, finding the right mentor is about creating a partnership that fosters growth. Their guidance can accelerate your journey towards wealth and success, helping you to cultivate the mindset needed to thrive in any economy. By actively seeking mentorship, you not only gain knowledge but also build a support system that can uplift you during challenging times. Remember, every great success story begins with a mentor who believed in the potential of their mentee.

The Benefits of Learning from Others

Learning from others is one of the most powerful tools for personal and financial growth. Throughout history, successful individuals have credited their achievements to the insights gained from mentors, books, and even casual conversations. For instance, the story of Thomas Edison highlights how he learned from failures and the experiences of others to invent the light bulb. By studying the paths of those who have succeeded before us, we can shortcut our journey and avoid unnecessary pitfalls.

The science behind learning from others is rooted in the concept of social learning theory, which posits that people can learn new behaviours by observing and imitating others. This principle is not just applicable in classrooms; it extends to business and personal finance as well. For example, Warren Buffet, one of the wealthiest individuals in the world, attributes much of his success to the lessons he learned from his mentor, Benjamin Graham. By understanding the principles that guided Graham's investment strategies, Buffet was able to refine his approach and build his empire.

To effectively learn from others, one must be open to feedback and willing to adapt. This means surrounding oneself with individuals who inspire and challenge you. Consider the journey of Oprah Winfrey, who often speaks about the mentors who have shaped her life. Her ability to absorb lessons from diverse perspectives has not only contributed to her success but has also enabled her to uplift millions through her platform. Engaging with those who have different experiences can provide insights that are crucial for personal and professional development.

Incorporating the habit of learning from others into your daily routine can be transformative. Start by reading biographies of successful people or attending seminars where industry leaders share their stories. Additionally, actively seek out conversations with individuals who have achieved what you aspire to. This can be as simple as reaching out for a coffee chat or joining networking groups. The step of actively engaging with others can lead to unexpected opportunities and valuable insights that can propel you forward.

Ultimately, the benefits of learning from others are manifold. It not only accelerates your journey towards success but also fosters a sense of community and shared growth. By embracing the wisdom and experiences of those around you, you can cultivate a mindset that is geared towards wealth and achievement. Remember, every successful individual was once a beginner who learned from the experiences of others, and by following in their footsteps, you too can achieve your financial goals.

Paying It Forward: Becoming a Mentor

In the journey towards wealth, the concept of mentoring often emerges as a vital component. Paying it forward by becoming a mentor not only enriches the lives of others but also deepens your own understanding and success. Consider the story of a successful entrepreneur who, after achieving great wealth, dedicated his time to guiding young innovators. His influence transformed their lives, while he found renewed purpose and satisfaction, illustrating that mentorship is a reciprocal relationship.

Science supports the notion that teaching and sharing knowledge reinforces one's own understanding and increases personal growth. Studies have shown that individuals who mentor others often experience heightened self-esteem and improved emotional intelligence. This phenomenon occurs because mentoring challenges you to clarify your thoughts and articulate your experiences effectively. It creates a cycle of learning, where both the mentor and mentee thrive, fostering a culture of success that extends beyond personal achievements.

To become an effective mentor, start by identifying your strengths and the areas where you can provide the most value. Reflect on your experiences and the lessons you've learned, as these stories will resonate with those you guide. Set clear goals for your mentoring relationships, focusing on what you wish to impart and what you hope to learn in return. Communication is key; be approachable and open to feedback, creating a safe space for your mentees to express their thoughts and challenges.

Additionally, consider the various formats in which mentoring can take place. Whether through formal programmes, casual meet-ups, or even online platforms, the essence of mentorship remains the same: sharing wisdom and experiences to uplift others. Incorporate practical steps into your mentoring approach, such as setting specific milestones for your mentees and celebrating their achievements. This not only motivates them but also reinforces their belief in their own potential.

Ultimately, becoming a mentor is not just about giving back; it's about creating a legacy of wealth and success that transcends individual accomplishments. As you invest in others, you contribute to a world where success is shared and multiplied. By embracing this role, you not only enhance your own millionaire mindset but also inspire a new generation to think, act, and grow rich in any economy, making the cycle of wealth and wisdom a continuous journey.

Chapter 9: Adapting to Economic Changes

Understanding Economic Cycles

Understanding economic cycles is essential for anyone aiming to build wealth, as these fluctuations can significantly impact financial decisions. Picture a small business owner, Tom, who experienced the highs of prosperity during an economic boom, only to face the harsh realities of a recession. His journey highlights how understanding these cycles can empower individuals to make informed choices, ensuring they remain resilient and adaptive in any economic climate.

Economic cycles, which consist of periods of expansion and contraction, are influenced by various factors including consumer behaviour, interest rates, and government policies. During expansion, people are more likely to spend, invest, and take risks, which can lead to increased wealth. However, during contractions, fear often prevails, causing individuals to hold back, which can further exacerbate economic downturns. This dynamic is illustrated by the story of Susan, a savvy investor who learned to recognise these shifts and adjusted her portfolio accordingly, ultimately thriving even during tough times.

Science supports the notion that individuals who understand economic cycles can better manage their finances. Research indicates that awareness of economic trends can lead to improved financial literacy and decision-making. For instance, studies show that people who prepare for downturns by saving or diversifying their investments are more likely to maintain their wealth. This principle can be applied by anyone willing to educate themselves about market trends and historical cycles, fostering a mindset geared towards success.

To navigate these economic fluctuations, there are actionable steps anyone can take. First, commit to ongoing education about economic indicators and trends. Second, develop a flexible financial strategy that can adapt to changing conditions. Lastly, build a network of like-minded individuals who can share insights and strategies. By following these steps, you will not only enhance your financial acumen but also cultivate the resilience needed to flourish in any economy.

In conclusion, understanding economic cycles is not merely an academic exercise; it is a vital skill for achieving financial success. Just as Tom and Susan learned through their experiences, recognising the patterns of expansion and contraction can empower you to make proactive financial decisions. Embrace the journey of learning and adapting, and you'll find that wealth can be built, regardless of the economic landscape.

Strategies for Thriving in Any Economy

In a world where economic fluctuations are the norm, developing strategies to thrive is essential. One key approach is cultivating a resilient mindset. This begins with the belief that challenges can lead to growth. For instance, consider the story of a small café owner who, during a recession, pivoted to a delivery model. By embracing change rather than resisting it, she not only survived but flourished, expanding her customer base.

Another effective strategy is to diversify income streams. Relying on a single source of income can be dangerous in unpredictable times. Think of a freelance graphic designer who, instead of solely depending on client work, started selling digital products online. This not only provided a safety net but also opened up new avenues for creativity and profit. It's about thinking outside the box and being adaptable.

Education and continuous learning play a vital role in thriving economically. Investing in knowledge can yield significant returns. The story of a young entrepreneur who took online courses during a downturn illustrates this perfectly. By enhancing her skills, she was able to launch a successful business that addressed emerging market needs. This highlights how being proactive in learning can equip you for future opportunities.

Networking and building relationships are also crucial strategies. Connecting with like-minded individuals can provide support and open doors to new ventures. A perfect example is a laid-off worker who, through networking events, found a mentor who guided him to start his own company. The power of community and collaboration cannot be underestimated; it can be the difference between stagnation and success.

Lastly, maintaining a positive cash flow is paramount. Implementing budgeting techniques and tracking expenses closely can help manage finances effectively. A real-life example is a small business owner who, by revising his financial strategies, managed to reduce costs and improve profitability. This disciplined approach to finances ensures that, regardless of economic conditions, one can remain resilient and ready to seize opportunities as they arise.

The Importance of Flexibility

Flexibility is a cornerstone of success in any economy. Many successful individuals have shared their stories of how adaptability has been the key to overcoming obstacles. For instance, consider the story of a once-struggling entrepreneur who, during a financial crisis, pivoted his business model to meet new market demands. This ability to shift gears not only saved his company but also led to unprecedented growth, showcasing the power of being open to change. Flexibility allows us to navigate through challenges and seize opportunities that others may overlook.

In the realm of science, numerous studies have shown that flexibility in thinking can lead to better problem-solving outcomes. Cognitive flexibility, which refers to the mental ability to switch between thinking about different concepts, is crucial for innovation. Research indicates that individuals who embrace change and adapt their strategies are more likely to succeed. This is evident in industries that evolve rapidly, requiring professionals to continuously learn and adapt to new technologies and processes. By fostering a flexible mindset, we can enhance our capacity for growth and success.

The steps to cultivating flexibility begin with a willingness to step out of one's comfort zone. This might involve learning new skills or embracing new perspectives. Each step taken to challenge oneself can lead to significant personal and professional growth. For example, a business leader who regularly seeks feedback from diverse team members demonstrates flexibility and a commitment to improvement. Such actions not only improve decision-making but also foster a culture of collaboration and innovation within an organisation.

Moreover, flexibility is essential for maintaining resilience in the face of adversity. Life is unpredictable, and the ability to adapt to changing circumstances can make all the difference. Those who can adjust their plans and strategies in response to setbacks are often the ones who emerge stronger. Take, for instance, the story of a family business that faced a sudden market downturn. Instead of succumbing to despair, they re-evaluated their offerings and introduced new products that better met their customers' needs. This not only saved the business but also positioned it for future success.

In conclusion, the importance of flexibility cannot be overstated. It is a vital habit that can significantly impact our journey towards wealth and success. By embracing change, being open to new ideas, and continually adapting our strategies, we can cultivate a millionaire mindset. Remember, flexibility is not just about reacting to change; it's about anticipating it and positioning ourselves to thrive, regardless of the economic climate.

Chapter 10: Creating Multiple Income Streams

Exploring Passive Income Opportunities

In the quest for financial freedom, exploring passive income opportunities can be a game changer. Imagine waking up every morning to find that your bank account has grown overnight without you lifting a finger. This isn't just a dream; it's a reality for those who understand the power of passive income. Whether it's through investments in real estate, dividend stocks, or creating digital products, the avenues are numerous and accessible to anyone willing to learn and take action.

Consider the story of Sarah, a single mother who turned her life around by investing in rental properties. With a modest savings, she purchased her first home, which she rented out. The steady stream of rental income allowed her to pay off debts and eventually buy more properties. Sarah's journey illustrates that passive income isn't reserved for the wealthy; it's achievable for anyone with determination and the right strategies.

Science backs the effectiveness of passive income as a wealth-building strategy as well. Research shows that individuals with multiple income streams tend to have higher financial stability and lower stress levels. By diversifying income sources, you not only buffer against economic downturns but also create a safety net that can support your lifestyle. This concept is not just theoretical; it's a practical approach that empowers individuals to take control of their financial futures.

If you're ready to embark on this journey, start by assessing your skills and interests. What can you create or invest in that aligns with your passions? Setting clear, actionable goals will help you stay focused. Begin small; even a modest investment can yield significant returns over time. Remember, the key is consistency and a willingness to adapt as you learn what works best for you.

Ultimately, exploring passive income opportunities is about changing your mindset. Embrace the idea that wealth is not merely about hard work but about smart work. As you cultivate the habits of successful individuals, you'll find that financial freedom is not just a possibility; it's a likely outcome. Let the stories of others inspire you, but more importantly, let your actions pave the way for your own success.

Diversifying Your Investments

Diversifying your investments is not just a strategy; it is a mindset that can lead to lasting wealth and financial stability. Imagine standing at the edge of a vast ocean, where each wave represents a different investment opportunity. By not putting all your eggs in one basket, you open yourself to the myriad of possibilities that the financial world has to offer. This approach not only mitigates risks but also enables growth in various market conditions, ensuring that your wealth continues to expand regardless of economic fluctuations.

Consider the story of Sarah, an entrepreneur who built her fortune through diversification. Starting with a small online retail business, she quickly realised that relying solely on one revenue stream was risky. By investing in real estate, stocks, and even emerging technologies, she created a safety net that allowed her to weather economic downturns. When her retail business faced challenges, her other investments sustained her lifestyle and provided her with the capital needed to pivot and adapt her business model.

The science behind diversification is rooted in the principle of risk management. Research shows that a well-diversified portfolio can reduce volatility and enhance returns over time. According to financial experts, having a mix of asset classes—such as equities, bonds, and alternative investments—can lead to more consistent performance. By understanding your risk tolerance and investment goals, you can strategically allocate your resources to create a balanced portfolio that aligns with your financial aspirations.

To start diversifying your investments, consider the following steps. First, assess your current financial situation and identify areas for growth. Next, research various investment vehicles, such as index funds, real estate, or commodities. It's crucial to educate yourself about the risks and benefits associated with each option. Finally, regularly review and adjust your portfolio to ensure it remains aligned with your evolving goals and market conditions.

Remember, successful investing is not a one-time event but a continuous journey. As you diversify your investments, embrace the mindset of adaptability and resilience. Just like a tree that grows stronger with each season, your financial foundation will become more robust as you learn and evolve in your investment strategies. By cultivating a diversified portfolio, you are not just protecting your wealth; you are actively participating in the journey towards financial independence and success.

Building a Business that Scales

Building a business that scales requires a mindset shift, one that embraces the potential for growth and the willingness to take calculated risks. Consider the story of a young entrepreneur who started a small online store selling handmade crafts. Initially, her sales were modest, but she soon realised that by leveraging social media and creating a compelling brand narrative, she could reach a global audience. This pivotal moment marked the beginning of her journey towards scaling her business, demonstrating how vision and strategy can transform a small venture into a thriving enterprise.

The science behind scaling a business lies in understanding the systems and processes that facilitate growth. Research indicates that companies with well-defined operational systems are more likely to experience sustainable growth. For instance, the young entrepreneur implemented a customer relationship management system that streamlined her interactions with clients. This not only improved customer satisfaction but also allowed her to focus on strategic decisions rather than getting bogged down in day-to-day operations. Such systems are essential in creating a scalable business model.

Another critical aspect is the development of a growth mindset. Adopting this mindset encourages business owners to view challenges as opportunities rather than obstacles. When the entrepreneur faced supply chain issues, instead of succumbing to frustration, she sought alternative suppliers and diversified her product range. This adaptability not only resolved her immediate problems but also positioned her business for future growth. Embracing a growth mindset allows entrepreneurs to navigate the complexities of scaling effectively.

Networking and collaboration play significant roles in building a scalable business. The entrepreneur sought mentorship from seasoned business leaders, which provided her with invaluable insights into market trends and effective strategies. Furthermore, she collaborated with other small businesses to create bundled offerings, which expanded her reach and customer base. These relationships foster a supportive ecosystem that is vital for sustained growth and innovation in any industry.

Finally, it is essential to maintain a strong focus on customer needs. Listening to customer feedback and adapting products accordingly can lead to increased loyalty and word-of-mouth referrals. The entrepreneur regularly engaged her customers through surveys and social media interactions, ensuring her offerings remained relevant. By prioritising customer satisfaction, she built a loyal community that not only supported her business but also advocated for it, propelling her towards greater success. In conclusion, building a business that scales is a multifaceted endeavour that requires vision, systems, a growth mindset, collaboration, and a steadfast commitment to understanding customer needs.

Chapter 11: The Mindset of Giving

The Impact of Generosity on Wealth

Generosity is often perceived as a selfless act, yet it has profound implications on personal wealth. Numerous studies have shown that individuals who engage in acts of kindness and share their resources tend to experience greater financial success. This phenomenon can be attributed to the positive mindset that generosity fosters. When people give, they often receive in return, not just in material wealth, but also in opportunities and connections that can lead to greater financial prosperity.

One powerful story that exemplifies this principle is that of a successful entrepreneur who made a habit of giving back to his community. Despite his initial struggles, he dedicated a portion of his profits to local charities and initiatives. Over time, his business flourished, and he attributed much of his success to the relationships and goodwill he built through his acts of generosity. This narrative highlights how investing in others can yield significant returns, creating a cycle of abundance.

Science supports the idea that generosity can enhance one's financial standing. Research indicates that giving activates the brain's reward centre, releasing dopamine, which not only makes us feel good but also encourages us to act in ways that are beneficial for our success. When we engage in generous behaviours, we are more likely to build networks and trust with others, paving the way for new business ventures and collaborations.

To cultivate a mindset of generosity, consider implementing small but impactful steps in your daily life. Start by volunteering your time, sharing your expertise, or even providing financial support to those in need. Each act of generosity creates a ripple effect, inspiring others to do the same and establishing a culture of abundance. This mindset shift can transform your relationship with money, allowing you to see it as a tool for creating positive change rather than merely a means to an end.

Ultimately, the impact of generosity on wealth is undeniable. By embracing a spirit of giving, we not only enrich the lives of others but also enhance our own financial journeys. In a world that often prioritises self-interest, choosing to be generous can set you apart, leading to unexpected opportunities and a wealthier, more fulfilling life. Embrace the billion-dollar habit of generosity, and watch your wealth, both financial and personal, flourish.

Philanthropy and Business Success

Philanthropy is not just a noble pursuit; it is a powerful driver of business success. When companies engage in charitable activities, they cultivate a positive brand image that resonates with consumers. For instance, consider the story of TOMS Shoes, which built its empire on the principle of giving back. With every pair of shoes sold, a new pair is donated to a child in need. This unique approach not only captured the hearts of customers but also significantly boosted sales, demonstrating that a commitment to philanthropy can lead to remarkable financial success.

Moreover, studies have shown that businesses that invest in social responsibility tend to outperform their competitors. Research from Harvard Business School indicates that companies with strong corporate social responsibility (CSR) practices enjoy higher levels of employee satisfaction and retention. A notable example is Salesforce, a company that integrates philanthropy into its business model. By providing employees with paid time off to volunteer, Salesforce fosters a culture of giving that enhances productivity and morale, resulting in sustained growth and profitability.

Adopting a philanthropic mindset can also inspire innovative business strategies. For example, Patagonia, the outdoor clothing brand, has committed to environmental activism as part of its core mission. By aligning its products with social causes, Patagonia not only attracts environmentally conscious consumers but also differentiates itself in a saturated market. This alignment of values creates a loyal customer base that is willing to pay a premium for products that reflect their beliefs, showcasing how integrating philanthropy can be a strategic advantage.

To implement a successful philanthropic strategy, businesses should start by identifying causes that resonate with their brand values. This alignment ensures authenticity and fosters deeper connections with consumers. Companies can engage in various forms of giving, from donating a portion of profits to supporting local communities through volunteer initiatives. By taking these steps, businesses can create a culture of giving that benefits both society and their bottom line.

Ultimately, the relationship between philanthropy and business success is symbiotic. As companies invest in their communities, they not only enhance their reputation but also unlock new avenues for growth. By embracing the philosophy that giving back is integral to success, businesses can cultivate a millionaire mindset that thrives in any economy. In this way, philanthropy becomes not just an act of kindness but a cornerstone of sustainable business practice.

Creating a Legacy Through Giving

Creating a legacy through giving is one of the most profound ways to make a lasting impact on the world. Many successful individuals have discovered that wealth is not merely a measure of material possessions but rather the ability to influence lives positively. Consider the story of Andrew Carnegie, who, after accumulating immense wealth through steel, dedicated his later years to philanthropic efforts, establishing libraries and educational institutions. His belief was clear: true success lies in what we give back to society, allowing others to benefit from our achievements.

Research supports the idea that generous giving enhances our own well-being. Studies have shown that acts of kindness and philanthropy can lead to improved mental health and increased happiness. This phenomenon, often referred to as the 'helper's high', illustrates how our brains release endorphins when we contribute to the welfare of others. By creating a legacy through giving, we not only uplift those around us but also enrich our own lives in the process. It's a reciprocal relationship that fosters community and personal growth.

To build a legacy through giving, one must first identify their passions and the causes that resonate most deeply with them. This can involve reflecting on personal experiences or witnessing the struggles of others. For instance, someone who has benefited from educational opportunities may choose to invest in scholarships for underprivileged youth. By aligning charitable efforts with personal values, individuals can ensure that their contributions have a meaningful impact.

Moreover, establishing a structured giving plan can amplify your legacy. This can include setting aside a percentage of income specifically for charitable donations or creating a foundation to support ongoing initiatives. Engaging in community projects or partnering with established organisations can also maximise the effectiveness of your contributions. Each step taken towards systematic giving can transform an ordinary act into a powerful legacy that inspires future generations.

Ultimately, creating a legacy through giving is about fostering a culture of generosity and compassion. As we share our wealth, knowledge, and time, we inspire others to do the same. This ripple effect can create a more equitable society, where everyone has the opportunity to thrive. In the end, the true measure of success lies not in what we accumulate but in what we give away, leaving a legacy that transcends our lifetime and touches countless lives.

Chapter 12: Maintaining Wealth and Success

Strategies for Sustaining Financial Growth

Sustaining financial growth requires a blend of strategic planning and a resilient mindset. One of the most effective strategies is to establish a robust financial plan that encompasses budgeting, saving, and investing. For instance, consider the story of a young entrepreneur who meticulously tracked her expenses and set clear savings goals. By doing so, she was not only able to build an emergency fund but also to invest in her business during crucial times. This habit of financial discipline is essential for anyone looking to maintain growth in any economy.

Another key strategy is to continuously educate yourself about financial markets and investment opportunities. Science shows that knowledge can significantly enhance decision-making capabilities. Take the example of a couple who spent a few hours each week learning about stock trading. Their commitment to understanding market trends allowed them to make informed investments, leading to substantial returns over time. This emphasis on financial literacy is critical, as it empowers individuals to navigate the complexities of wealth accumulation.

Networking is also a powerful tool for sustaining financial growth. Building relationships with like-minded individuals can lead to opportunities that may not be available otherwise. A poignant example is a business owner who attended local meetups and connected with other entrepreneurs. Through these connections, he gained insights into successful strategies and even partnered with others to expand his business reach. Creating a supportive network can significantly enhance one's ability to thrive financially.

Diversification is another vital strategy to consider. By spreading investments across various assets, individuals can minimise risk and increase their chances of sustaining growth. A story that illustrates this is that of an investor who started with a single stock. After facing a loss, he diversified his portfolio by including bonds and real estate. This shift not only protected his investments but also led to consistent growth over the years. Embracing diversification can be a game-changer for anyone serious about financial stability.

Finally, consistency is the bedrock of sustained financial growth. Developing habits such as regular saving and investing can lead to significant wealth over time. A relatable story is that of a man who set up automatic transfers to his savings account. This simple act resulted in a substantial nest egg that enabled him to start a business. By committing to consistent actions, individuals can create a pathway towards financial independence, regardless of economic conditions.

Continuous Learning and Adaptation

In today's fast-paced world, continuous learning and adaptation are not just advantageous; they are essential for success. Consider the story of a small business owner who, once thriving, found their sales dwindling due to changing market dynamics. Instead of resisting these changes, they embraced them by learning new digital marketing strategies and adapting their business model. This willingness to learn not only revived their business but also set them on a path of sustained growth, demonstrating that adaptability is a key trait in the millionaire mindset.

Scientific research backs up the importance of continuous learning. Studies show that engaging in lifelong learning can lead to better problem-solving skills and increased creativity. For example, a study conducted at the University of California found that individuals who actively seek out new knowledge are more likely to adapt successfully to changing environments. This scientific evidence reinforces the idea that cultivating a habit of learning can directly influence our ability to thrive in any economy.

To develop a mindset geared towards continuous learning, one can start by setting specific goals. For instance, dedicating just 30 minutes a day to read books or articles related to your field can yield significant benefits over time. Furthermore, attending workshops or online courses can provide new insights and skills. By taking these small, consistent steps, anyone can create a solid foundation for lifelong learning and adaptation.

Another powerful story comes from the tech industry, where giants like IBM and Microsoft have consistently reinvented themselves. They have embraced the need for adaptation by investing heavily in research and development. This dedication to learning has allowed them to stay ahead of their competitors and remain relevant in a rapidly changing technological landscape. Their success reinforces the notion that continuous learning is not just an individual endeavour but a corporate strategy that can lead to monumental success.

In conclusion, the habit of continuous learning and adaptation is invaluable for anyone looking to cultivate a millionaire mindset. By recognising the importance of staying informed and flexible, individuals can navigate the complexities of modern economics with confidence. Remember, the journey to wealth is not solely about financial acumen; it's also about a commitment to growth and the willingness to evolve with the world around us.

The Importance of Gratitude and Reflection

Gratitude is more than just a fleeting emotion; it is a powerful practice that can transform our lives and minds. Numerous studies have shown that regularly expressing gratitude can lead to increased happiness and reduced stress, significantly impacting our overall well-being. For instance, individuals who maintain gratitude journals report feeling more optimistic and satisfied with their lives. This simple act of reflection can set a positive tone for our daily experiences, allowing us to focus on what we have rather than what we lack.

Reflecting on our achievements and experiences also plays a crucial role in personal growth. When we take the time to look back on our successes, we cultivate a deeper understanding of our journey. This reflection not only boosts our confidence but also provides valuable insights into the strategies that work for us. Consider the story of a successful entrepreneur who, after facing several failures, began to document his achievements. By revisiting his past victories, he was able to identify patterns that led to his eventual success, demonstrating the importance of self-reflection in achieving our goals.

Gratitude and reflection can be integrated into our daily routines through simple yet effective steps. One approach is to set aside a few moments each day for reflection, perhaps during a morning coffee or before bedtime. This practice can include jotting down three things you are grateful for or reviewing your accomplishments from the day. Over time, this habit can rewire your brain to focus on the positive, fostering a mindset that attracts more opportunities and success.

The science behind gratitude is compelling, with research indicating that it can lead to improved physical health, better sleep, and even enhanced relationships. When we express gratitude, our brain releases neurotransmitters like dopamine and serotonin, which are associated with feelings of happiness and contentment. This physiological response highlights the connection between our mindset and our overall well-being, reinforcing the idea that cultivating gratitude can indeed lead to a wealthier mindset in both personal and financial realms.

In conclusion, the practice of gratitude and reflection is a billion-dollar habit that anyone can adopt. It lays the foundation for a positive mindset, essential for achieving success in any economy. By acknowledging our blessings and reflecting on our journeys, we not only enhance our mental and emotional well-being but also open the door to greater opportunities and wealth. Embrace gratitude and make reflection a part of your daily life, and watch how it transforms your approach to success and prosperity. It's a beautiful day

www.ingramcontent.com/pod-product-compliance
Lightning Source LLC
Chambersburg PA
CBHW070540130626
46555CB00003B/1503